Funding The Problems So, Make It a Problem!

By

Melvin Prince Johnakin

Funding The Problems, So Make It A Problem!

Copyright 2024 by Melvin Prince Johnakin

All rights reserved. No part of this publication may be reproduced, distributed, or transmitted in any form or by any means, including photocopying, recording, or other electronic or mechanical methods, without the prior written permission of the publisher, except in the case of brief quotations embodied in critical reviews and certain other noncommercial uses permitted by copyright law.

Although the author and publisher have made every effort to ensure that the information in this book was correct at press time, the author and publisher do not assume and hereby disclaim any liability to any party for any loss, damage, or disruption caused by errors or omissions, whether such errors or omissions result from negligence, accident, or any other cause. Adherence to all applicable laws and regulations, including international, federal, state, and local governing professional licensing, business practices, advertising, and all other aspects of doing business in the US, Canada or any other jurisdiction is the sole responsibility of the reader and consumer.

Neither the author nor the publisher assumes any responsibility or liability whatsoever on behalf of the consumer or reader of this material. Any perceived slight of any individual or organization is purely unintentional.

The resources in this book are provided for informational purposes only and should not be used to replace the specialized training and professional judgment of a health care or mental health care professional. Neither the author nor the publisher can be held responsible for the use of the information provided within this book. Please always consult a trained professional before making any decision regarding treatment of yourself or others.

Foreword

In an age where financial literacy is often overshadowed by the complexities of modern economies, "Funding Problems" by Melvin Prince Johnakin emerges as a beacon of clarity and insight. This book is not just a compilation of strategies and solutions; it is a comprehensive guide that delves into the intricate labyrinth of funding challenges faced by individuals, startups, and established businesses alike.

Melvin's expertise in finance, coupled with his unique ability to articulate complex concepts in an accessible manner, makes this book an essential read for anyone seeking to navigate the tumultuous waters of funding. From the outset, he draws readers in with relatable anecdotes and real-world examples, illuminating the myriad obstacles that can impede access to capital. Yet rather than merely highlighting these issues, Melvin offers practical solutions, actionable insights, and a roadmap for overcoming the funding hurdles that so many encounter.

What sets "Funding Problems" apart is its holistic approach. Melvin understands that funding is not just about money; it's about vision, strategy, resilience, and most importantly, the human element. He emphasizes the importance of building relationships with potential investors and stakeholders, fostering a sense of community and collaboration that is essential for success in today's interconnected world. His insights on the significance of storytelling in pitching ideas are particularly noteworthy. In a landscape where countless proposals vie for attention, Melvin's advice on crafting a compelling narrative can be the difference between success and failure.

Moreover, this book transcends traditional financial advice by addressing the psychological aspects of funding. Melvin skillfully navigates the emotional rollercoaster that often accompanies the quest for financial backing, providing readers with valuable tools to maintain their motivation and resilience in the face of adversity. His candid discussions about his own experiences with funding challenges lend authenticity to his guidance, allowing readers to connect with him on a personal level.

As you embark on this journey through "Funding Problems," you will find not only a wealth of knowledge but also a mentor in Melvin. His passion for empowering others is palpable on every page, and his unwavering belief in the potential of individuals and businesses to overcome financial obstacles is truly inspiring. I encourage you to dive deep into these pages, absorb the lessons, and apply them to your own endeavors. Whether you are an entrepreneur, a student, or simply someone interested in understanding the financial landscape better, this book will equip you with the tools you need to succeed.

In conclusion, I wholeheartedly recommend "Funding Problems" to anyone who seeks to demystify the funding process. Melvin Prince Johnakin has crafted a remarkable resource that will not only inform but also inspire you to take charge of your financial destiny. Let this book be your guide as you navigate the challenges ahead, and may it empower you to turn your funding problems into opportunities.

Acknowledgments

Writing a book is a journey that requires not only dedication and hard work but also the support of countless individuals who believe in the vision. As I reflect on the creation of "Funding Problems," I am filled with gratitude for those who have played pivotal roles in bringing this project to fruition.

First and foremost, I would like to express my heartfelt thanks to my family. Your unwavering support and encouragement have been my anchor throughout this process. To my partner, who has been my sounding board and my greatest cheerleader, your belief in my abilities has fueled my passion and determination. Thank you for your patience during those late nights and early mornings spent writing and revising.

I am especially grateful to my mentors and colleagues in the finance industry who have generously shared their wisdom and experiences with me. Your insights have not only enriched my understanding of funding challenges but have also inspired me to delve deeper into this subject.

I also want to acknowledge the many entrepreneurs, business owners, and innovators who shared their stories with me. Your candidness in discussing the struggles and triumphs of securing funding has enriched this book immeasurably. It is your experiences that have shaped the narrative and provided real-world context to the strategies outlined herein. Thank you for trusting me with your stories.

To the readers, thank you for choosing to embark on this journey with me. Your interest and engagement with these ideas are what ultimately drive me to write. I hope that "Funding Problems" resonates with you and serves as a valuable resource as you navigate your own funding challenges.

Lastly, I would like to extend my gratitude to the broader community of writers and thought leaders whose work has influenced my thinking. Your dedication to sharing knowledge and fostering dialogue inspires me to contribute my voice to the conversation.

As I close this acknowledgment, I am reminded that the journey of writing a book is never undertaken alone. It is a collective endeavor, and I am deeply thankful for each person who has been a part of this process. May the insights contained in "Funding Problems" empower you to tackle the challenges ahead and turn your aspirations into reality. Thank you for joining me on this journey.

Introduction

In contemporary society, the funding landscape plays a crucial role in shaping our communities, economies, and overall societal structures. The allocation of funds influences various sectors, from education and healthcare to infrastructure and social services. Understanding this landscape is essential not only for policymakers and organizations seeking financial support but also for individuals who are affected by these funding decisions. This introduction will explore the key themes of funding allocation, its societal implications, and the interconnectedness of various funding issues, providing a comprehensive overview of the contemporary funding landscape.

The funding landscape is multidimensional, encompassing public and private sources of finance. Governments, philanthropic organizations, and private investors all contribute to the pool of available funds. Each of these entities has distinct motivations and priorities that shape how funds are allocated. For instance, government funding is often directed toward programs that aim to enhance public welfare, such as healthcare and education. In contrast, private investors may focus on initiatives that promise financial returns or social impact.

The current funding environment is characterized by a growing emphasis on accountability and transparency. Stakeholders are increasingly demanding evidence of effective fund use, leading to a shift in how organizations report and evaluate their impact. This trend reflects a broader societal expectation that funds should not only be allocated efficiently but also used to generate meaningful outcomes.

The allocation of funds is perhaps the most critical aspect of the funding landscape. It determines which projects receive financial support and, consequently, shapes the trajectory of various sectors. Fund allocation is influenced by a variety of factors, including political priorities, market trends, and societal needs. For example, in the wake of the COVID-19 pandemic, many governments redirected funds to healthcare and social services, highlighting the importance of adaptability in funding strategies.

Moreover, the allocation process often reveals underlying societal values and priorities. For instance, funding disparities can indicate systemic inequalities, with marginalized communities frequently receiving less financial support. This inequity raises important questions about the fairness of funding distribution and challenges policymakers to address these disparities.

The implications of funding allocation extend far beyond mere financial transactions; they affect the very fabric of society. When funds are directed toward specific programs or initiatives, they can catalyze significant change. For instance, increased funding for education can lead to improved academic outcomes, while investments in renewable energy can stimulate economic growth and environmental sustainability.

Conversely, inadequate funding can hamper progress and exacerbate existing social issues. For example, underfunded healthcare systems may struggle to provide adequate services, leading to negative health outcomes for vulnerable populations. These scenarios highlight the critical nature of funding decisions and their far-reaching consequences.

Furthermore, the societal implications of funding extend to the way communities perceive and engage with their governments and institutions. When funding is allocated transparently and equitably, trust in public institutions can grow. Conversely, opaque funding processes can lead to disillusionment and decreased civic engagement. Thus, the manner in which funds are allocated can either reinforce or undermine social cohesion.

Another important theme to consider is the interconnectedness of various funding issues. Funding is rarely isolated to a single sector or initiative; rather, it often intersects with multiple areas of society. For example, investments in education can have downstream effects on economic development, public health, and social equity. Similarly, funding for infrastructure projects can influence community well-being, accessibility, and environmental sustainability.

This interconnectedness presents both opportunities and challenges. On one hand, it allows for holistic approaches to problem-solving, where funding can be strategically directed to address multiple societal issues simultaneously. For instance, a comprehensive funding strategy that supports education, healthcare, and job training can create a more resilient workforce and improve overall community health.

On the other hand, the complexity of these interconnections can make it difficult to navigate funding landscapes. Policymakers and organizations must consider the ripple effects of their funding decisions, which may require collaboration across sectors and stakeholders. This necessity for collaboration underscores the importance of communication and partnership in the funding process.

In conclusion, the funding landscape in contemporary society is a dynamic and multifaceted arena that significantly influences various aspects of life. The allocation of funds, societal implications, and the interconnectedness of funding issues are key themes that underscore the importance of understanding this landscape. As society continues to evolve, the need for effective and equitable funding strategies will only grow in importance. Policymakers, organizations, and individuals must work together to navigate this complex landscape, ensuring that funds are allocated in ways that promote social equity, economic development, and overall community well-being. By fostering transparency, accountability, and collaboration, we can create a funding environment that serves the best interests of all members of society, paving the way for a more equitable and prosperous future.

Chapter 1

The Overcrowded Prison Crisis

The issue of overcrowded prisons has reached a critical point in many countries around the world. This chapter delves into the current state of prison overcrowding, examining its causes, consequences, and the Implications for inmates and society. Through a combination of statistics, case studies, and a discussion of the financial burden on taxpayers, we aim to shed light on this pressing crisis.

Prison overcrowding is a multifaceted issue that affects various aspects of the criminal justice system. As of recent reports, many countries face significant challenges in managing their prison populations. For instance, the United States has one of the highest incarceration rates globally, with an estimated 2.3 million individuals behind bars. According to the Bureau of Justice Statistics, more than 60% of state prisons are operating at or above capacity.

In countries like Brazil and the Philippines, the situation is similarly dire. Brazilian prisons are notoriously overcrowded, with some facilities housing three times their intended capacity. The Philippine government has acknowledged that their prison system is overwhelmed, with inmates often living in inhumane conditions. The problem is not confined to these nations; many European countries are also grappling with rising prison populations, often exacerbated by harsh sentencing laws and a lack of effective rehabilitation programs.

Several factors contribute to the rising prison population:

1. Harsh Sentencing Laws: Mandatory minimum sentences for non-violent offenses, particularly drug-related crimes, have led to longer sentences and increased incarceration rates.

2. Recidivism: A lack of effective rehabilitation programs and support systems for released inmates often leads to repeat offenses, perpetuating the cycle of incarceration.

3. War on Drugs: Policies aimed at combating drug-related crimes have significantly increased the number of individuals imprisoned for drug offenses, further straining prison resources.

4. Socioeconomic Factors: High poverty rates, lack of education, and limited access to mental health services contribute to criminal behavior, resulting in higher arrest and incarceration rates.

The consequences of overcrowded prisons extend beyond mere numbers; they profoundly affect the lives of inmates.

Overcrowded facilities often experience higher rates of violence among inmates. The lack of personal space can lead to heightened tensions and conflicts, resulting in fights, assaults, and sometimes even homicides. According to a study by the Vera Institute of Justice, prisons operating at or above capacity report significantly higher rates of inmate-on-inmate violence.

The psychological impact of overcrowding cannot be overstated. Inmates often face heightened levels of stress, anxiety, and depression due to the cramped living conditions and lack of privacy. A report by the National Institute of Mental Health found that individuals incarcerated in overcrowded conditions are more likely to experience severe mental health issues, which can exacerbate the challenges they face upon re-entry into society.

Overcrowding severely limits inmates' access to essential services, including healthcare, educational programs, and vocational training. In many cases, inmates are unable to receive adequate medical care due to the sheer number of individuals requiring attention. According to a report by the Bureau of Justice Assistance, prisoners in overcrowded facilities often wait weeks or even months for necessary medical treatment.

Incarceration affects not only the individual but also their families and communities. Overcrowded prisons can lead to longer sentences, making it difficult for inmates to maintain relationships with their loved ones. This disruption can have lasting effects on families, particularly children, who may experience emotional and financial hardships as a result of a parent's incarceration.

The consequences of prison overcrowding extend beyond the walls of correctional facilities and have significant implications for society as a whole.

While the primary goal of incarceration is to protect society, overcrowded prisons can undermine this objective. High recidivism rates and a lack of rehabilitation programs mean that many inmates are released back into society without the necessary skills or support to avoid re-offending. A study by the Pew Charitable Trusts found that nearly 70% of released prisoners are rearrested within three years, highlighting the failure of the prison system to effectively rehabilitate offenders.

The financial implications of overcrowded prisons are stark. Maintaining overcrowded facilities is costly, and taxpayers bear the brunt of these expenses. The average cost of incarcerating an individual in the U.S. is approximately $31,000 per year. This figure does not account for the additional costs associated with increased violence, medical care, and the need for additional staff to manage the overcrowded conditions.

In states like California, the financial strain has led to significant budget reallocations, with funds diverted from education and healthcare to support the prison system. The California Legislative Analyst's Office reported that the state spends over $12 billion annually on its prison system, a number that continues to rise as overcrowding persists.

Prison overcrowding can also erode public trust in the justice system. When individuals see that prisons are unable to provide rehabilitation and are instead breeding grounds for violence and despair, confidence in the system diminishes. This erosion can lead to calls for reform, but it can also foster cynicism and a belief that the justice system is fundamentally flawed.

California's prison system has faced severe overcrowding for decades. In 2006, the U.S. Supreme Court ruled that the state's prisons were unconstitutionally overcrowded, violating the Eighth Amendment's prohibition against cruel and unusual punishment. The ruling mandated that California reduce its prison population by approximately 40,000 inmates. This led to a series of reforms, including the implementation of realignment policies that shifted low-level offenders to county jails and increased funding for rehabilitation programs.

While these reforms have shown some success in reducing overcrowding, challenges remain. The state still grapples with high recidivism rates and ongoing debates about the adequacy of mental health services for inmates.

Brazil's prison system is one of the most overcrowded in the world, with facilities operating at nearly 170% of their capacity. Inmates are often subjected to inhumane conditions, including extreme violence and unsanitary living conditions. The Brazilian government has acknowledged these issues, yet solutions remain elusive.

In response to public outcry, Brazil has attempted to implement reforms to decriminalize certain offenses and promote alternative sentencing. However, progress has been slow, and the situation remains critical. The Brazilian experience highlights the complexity of addressing prison overcrowding and the need for comprehensive reforms that address root causes, such as poverty and lack of access to education.

The Philippines has faced a significant prison crisis, particularly following President Rodrigo Duterte's controversial war on drugs, which led to a surge in arrests and convictions. Many facilities in the Philippines are now operating at over 400% capacity, with inmates living in deplorable conditions. The government has recognized the need for reform, but challenges such as corruption and limited resources hinder progress.

In response, various non-governmental organizations have stepped in to provide support, including legal assistance and rehabilitation programs. These efforts underscore the importance of community involvement in addressing the challenges of prison overcrowding.

The crisis of overcrowded prisons is a complex issue that demands immediate attention from policymakers, advocates, and society as a whole. The statistics and case studies presented in this chapter reveal the profound impact of overcrowding on inmates and the broader community, highlighting the urgent need for comprehensive reforms.

Addressing prison overcrowding requires a multifaceted approach that includes sentencing reform, increased funding for rehabilitation programs, and a commitment to addressing the underlying social issues that contribute to crime. Only through concerted efforts can we hope to alleviate the burden of overcrowded prisons and create a more just and effective criminal justice system. As society grapples with this crisis, it is essential to remember that the ultimate goal should be rehabilitation, not punishment, paving the way for individuals to reintegrate into society and contribute positively to their communities.

Chapter 2

The Business of Incarceration

The privatization of prisons represents a significant shift in the landscape of the criminal justice system, introducing profit motives into what is traditionally a public service. As the number of incarcerated individuals continues to rise, the role of private prison companies has become increasingly prominent. This chapter explores the implications of privatization, analyzing how profit motives influence funding decisions, the impact on rehabilitation efforts, and the cyclical relationship between funding and incarceration rates.

The privatization of prisons began in the United States in the 1980s, coinciding with the "tough on crime" policies that led to a dramatic increase in incarceration rates. The first modern private prison, the Corrections Corporation of America (now Core Civic), opened in 1983, marking the beginning of a trend that would see private companies take over the management of correctional facilities across the nation.

The rationale behind privatization was rooted in the belief that private companies could operate prisons more efficiently and cost-effectively than the government. Proponents argued that competition would lead to better services, reduced costs, and increased innovation. However, the reality has often been far more complex.

Private prisons derive their revenue from contracts with state and federal governments, which pay per inmate. This creates a fundamental conflict of interest: the more inmates a private prison houses, the greater its profits. As a result, the business model encourages the incarceration of more individuals rather than focusing on rehabilitation and reduction of recidivism.

According to a report by the Justice Policy Institute, private prison companies spent over $1 million on lobbying and campaign contributions from 2010 to 2012 to influence legislation that would increase incarceration rates. This investment underscores the extent to which profit motives shape policy decisions, often at the expense of public safety and effective rehabilitation.

The introduction of private prisons has transformed how funding is allocated within the criminal justice system. In many cases, states prioritize funding for incarceration over rehabilitation and social services. A report from the Brennan Center for Justice highlights that states spend approximately three times more on prisons than on education.

This disparity is rooted in the profit-driven nature of private prisons. When funds are allocated to build and maintain correctional facilities, there is less available for programs that address the root causes of crime, such as mental health services, drug treatment programs, and educational opportunities. The emphasis on incarceration results in a system that perpetuates the cycle of crime rather than breaking it.

Private prison contracts often include provisions that incentivize states to maintain high occupancy rates. These contracts can include clauses that require states to keep a certain percentage of beds filled, leading to policies that promote longer sentences and limit alternatives to incarceration.

For example, in some states, private prison operators have lobbied for mandatory minimum sentencing laws, which have contributed to the increase in prison populations. This creates a feedback loop where the need for profit drives policy decisions that increase incarceration rates, further enriching private prison companies.

The focus on profit undermines the ability of private prisons to provide meaningful rehabilitation programs. Many private facilities allocate minimal resources to education, vocational training, and mental health services, prioritizing cost savings over the well-being of inmates. A 2016 report from the National Institute of Justice found that private prisons often provide fewer educational and vocational opportunities compared to their public counterparts.

Without access to these essential programs, inmates are less likely to develop the skills and support systems necessary for successful reintegration into society. This lack of rehabilitation contributes to high recidivism rates, reinforcing the cycle of incarceration and profit.

The privatization of prisons has created a system where incarceration is viewed as a revenue stream. As states struggle with budget constraints, the allure of cost savings from privatization can be tempting. However, this focus on short-term financial gains obscures the long-term societal costs of increased incarceration.

Research from the Vera Institute of Justice indicates that states that privatize their prison systems often experience increases in incarceration rates. The reliance on private companies to manage prisons can lead to a lack of accountability and oversight, resulting in conditions that may exacerbate the issues of violence, mental health crises, and recidivism.

The influence of private prison companies extends beyond budget allocations; it permeates the political landscape. Lobbying efforts by these companies have led to policy changes that favor their interests, often under the guise of public safety. For instance, the American Legislative Exchange Council (ALEC), a conservative nonprofit organization, has been instrumental in promoting legislation that increases incarceration rates, benefiting private prison operators.

The intertwining of corporate interests with public policy raises ethical questions about the motivations behind criminal justice reforms. When profit is prioritized over public safety and rehabilitation, the integrity of the justice system is compromised.

Arizona provides a compelling case study of the effects of privatization on incarceration rates and public policy. In the early 1990s, the state began contracting with private prison companies to manage its correctional facilities. Initially, the move was justified by claims of cost savings and improved efficiency.

However, a 2015 report from the Arizona Auditor General revealed that private prisons were not only more expensive than their public counterparts but also provided lower-quality services. The report indicated that private facilities had higher rates of inmate-on-inmate violence, inadequate healthcare, and fewer rehabilitation programs.

Despite these findings, the state continued to renew contracts with private prison companies, illustrating the cycle of funding and profit that had taken hold. The political influence of these companies, coupled with a lack of accountability, perpetuated a system that prioritized profit over the well-being of inmates and public safety.

The consequences of the profit-driven model of incarceration extend beyond financial implications; they have profound human costs. The prioritization of profit over rehabilitation has devastating effects on individuals, families, and communities.

Inmates in private prisons often face harsher conditions than those in public facilities. Reports of overcrowding, inadequate healthcare, and limited access to educational programs are common. The lack of investment in rehabilitation leads to a cycle of reoffending, further entrenching individuals in the criminal justice system.

For example, studies have shown that individuals released from private prisons are more likely to reoffend than those released from public facilities. This not only impacts the individuals involved but also places additional strain on families and communities, perpetuating cycles of poverty and crime.

The impact of privatized incarceration extends to families of inmates, who often face significant emotional and financial burdens. Families may struggle to maintain contact with incarcerated loved ones, particularly if they are housed far from home. The stigma associated with incarceration can also lead to social isolation and discrimination, further compounding the challenges faced by families.

Communities are affected as well. High incarceration rates disrupt social structures and contribute to economic instability. Neighborhoods with high rates of incarceration often experience increased poverty, decreased educational opportunities, and a lack of social cohesion, perpetuating cycles of disadvantage.

The challenges presented by the privatization of prisons highlight the urgent need for reform in the criminal justice system. A shift in focus from profit to rehabilitation is essential to address the underlying issues that contribute to crime and recidivism.

Policy Recommendations

1. Abolish Private Prisons: One of the most direct solutions to address the issues associated with privatization is to abolish private prisons altogether. Transitioning to a fully public system would eliminate the profit motive and allow for a focus on rehabilitation and public safety.

2. Increase Funding for Rehabilitation Programs: States should prioritize funding for educational and vocational training programs, mental health services, and substance abuse treatment. Investing in rehabilitation can reduce recidivism rates and ultimately lead to safer communities.

3. Implement Sentencing Reforms: Policymakers should consider reforms that reduce mandatory minimum sentences and provide alternatives to incarceration for non-violent offenses. Diversion programs and restorative justice initiatives can help address the root causes of crime while minimizing the reliance on incarceration.

4. Enhance Oversight and Accountability: Increased oversight of both public and private correctional facilities is essential to ensure the humane treatment of inmates. Regular audits, inspections, and accountability measures can help identify and rectify issues related to violence, healthcare, and rehabilitation.

5. Engage Communities in the Reform Process: Community involvement is critical to the success of criminal justice reforms. Engaging families, advocates, and local organizations can help create a more holistic approach to addressing the factors that contribute to crime and recidivism.

The business of incarceration represents a complex intersection of profit motives, public policy, and the human experience. The privatization of prisons has introduced significant challenges to the criminal justice system, prioritizing profit over rehabilitation and public safety. As the cycle of funding and incarceration rates continues, it is imperative that we advocate for reforms that prioritize the well-being of individuals and communities.

Addressing the crisis of incarceration requires a fundamental shift in how society views and manages crime. By moving away from a profit-driven model and embracing a focus on rehabilitation and restorative justice, we can create a more equitable and effective criminal justice system that serves the needs of all individuals. In doing so, we can begin to break the cycles of incarceration that have plagued our society for far too long.

Chapter 3

A Comparative Look: Funding Allocations

Funding allocations within government budgets reveal much about societal values and priorities. In recent decades, many governments have increasingly directed resources toward punitive measures, particularly in the realm of incarceration, while failing to adequately fund preventive solutions such as education, healthcare, and social services. This chapter provides an overview of government funding priorities, compares allocations for prisons with those for essential social services, and discusses the implications of prioritizing punitive measures over preventive solutions.

The shift in funding priorities can be traced back to the "War on Drugs" initiated in the 1980s in the United States, which led to policies emphasizing punishment rather than rehabilitation. This marked a turning point where the criminal justice system began to receive a disproportionate share of government budgets. As crime rates rose, public fear prompted lawmakers to enact harsher sentencing laws and allocate more resources to law enforcement and corrections.

In many cases, the rhetoric around crime and punishment dominated political discourse, resulting in policies designed to appear tough on crime. This focus obscured the importance of addressing underlying social issues that contribute to criminal behavior, such as poverty, lack of education, and inadequate healthcare.

Today, the fiscal landscape reflects a significant imbalance in funding allocations. For instance, in the United States, the Bureau of Justice Statistics reported that state and local governments spent approximately $300 billion on corrections in 2020. In contrast, funding for education and social services has not seen commensurate increases. According to the National Education Association, public education spending was about $760 billion in the same year, highlighting a significant disparity.

These figures reveal a systemic issue where punitive measures are prioritized over investments in human capital and community well-being. This chapter will delve deeper into the comparisons between these funding allocations and their long-term implications.

The funding allocation for prisons often overshadows that for education, despite the clear benefits of investing in the latter. A stark example can be seen in states like California, where prison spending has outpaced funding for K-12 education. The California Legislative Analyst's Office reported that the state spends about $12 billion annually on prisons, while K-12 education funding was approximately $76 billion.

This trend is not isolated to California; many states have faced similar challenges. The prioritization of prison funding over education has several implications:

1. Impact on Educational Outcomes: Underfunded public schools struggle to provide quality education, which can contribute to higher dropout rates and lower academic achievement. These outcomes correlate strongly with increased likelihood of incarceration, creating a vicious cycle.

2. Long-Term Economic Consequences: Investing in education has been shown to yield long-term economic benefits, including higher earning potential and reduced reliance on social services. Conversely, high incarceration rates can lead to economic stagnation in communities, as individuals face barriers to employment and education post-release.

Healthcare funding also suffers in comparison to corrections spending. The healthcare system in the U.S. faces significant challenges, including rising costs and lack of access for many individuals. In 2020, the National Health Expenditure Accounts reported that U.S. healthcare spending was approximately $4 trillion, but only a fraction of this amount is allocated to mental health and substance abuse treatment, areas that are crucial for addressing factors contributing to crime.

The implications of this disparity are profound:

1. Mental Health Crisis: Many individuals in the criminal justice system suffer from untreated mental health issues. A report from the Treatment Advocacy Center indicated that individuals with severe mental illnesses are more likely to be incarcerated than hospitalized. The

failure to invest in mental health care leads to a cycle where individuals who need help end up in prison rather than receiving appropriate treatment.

2. Substance Abuse Disorders: The criminal justice system often becomes the default response to substance abuse, with many individuals incarcerated for drug-related offenses. The National Institute on Drug Abuse found that only a small percentage of individuals with substance use disorders receive treatment. Increased funding for healthcare could address these issues proactively, reducing the number of individuals entering the prison system.

Social services, including housing assistance, job training programs, and community development initiatives, are critical components of a holistic approach to preventing crime. However, funding for these services often pales in comparison to corrections spending. For instance, the Center on Budget and Policy Priorities reported that funding for social services has been cut or stagnated in many states, while corrections budgets have continued to grow.

The implications of underfunding social services include:

1. Increased Poverty Rates: When social services are underfunded, communities experience higher rates of poverty, which is directly correlated with increased

crime rates. Economic hardship can lead individuals to engage in criminal behavior as a means of survival.

2. Lack of Support for At-Risk Youth: Insufficient funding for youth programs, mentorship, and after-school activities can leave young people vulnerable to gang involvement and criminal behavior. Investing in social services that support youth development can help mitigate these risks.

In Massachusetts, a stark contrast exists between funding for corrections and education. The Massachusetts Department of Correction reported spending approximately $1.4 billion on corrections in 2020, while the budget for the Department of Elementary and Secondary Education was about $1.2 billion. This indicates a nearly equal distribution of funds, yet the outcomes tell a different story.

Despite significant funding for corrections, recidivism rates remain high. The Massachusetts Executive Office of Public Safety and Security reported that about 40% of individuals released from prison are re-incarcerated within three years. This raises questions about the effectiveness of punitive measures versus the potential benefits of increased investment in education and rehabilitation programs.

Texas provides another illustrative example of funding disparities. The state has one of the largest prison systems in the country, with a budget of over $3 billion for corrections in 2020. In contrast, funding for public education was approximately $60 billion. The Texas Criminal Justice Coalition has highlighted that high incarceration rates do not correlate with lower crime rates; in fact, crime rates in Texas have remained relatively stable despite increasing prison populations.

The Texas experience demonstrates the futility of relying on incarceration as a primary means of addressing crime. By reallocating some of the significant funds directed toward corrections to education and social services, the state could invest in preventive measures that address the root causes of crime.

The preference for punitive measures over preventive solutions has far-reaching societal consequences. By focusing on incarceration, governments inadvertently perpetuate cycles of poverty, crime, and social disintegration.

The implications include:

1. Erosion of Trust in Government: Communities that experience high incarceration rates often feel abandoned by the government, leading to eroded trust in public institutions. This lack of trust can hinder effective community policing, making it more difficult to address crime collaboratively.

2. Increased Social Inequality: The criminal justice system disproportionately impacts marginalized communities, exacerbating existing social inequalities. When funding for education and social services is insufficient, these communities face compounded challenges, including poverty, unemployment, and lack of access to healthcare.

The economic implications of prioritizing incarceration over preventive measures are significant. High incarceration rates lead to:

1. Lost Economic Productivity: Incarceration removes individuals from the workforce, leading to lost productivity and economic potential. The National Institute of Justice estimates that the U.S. economy loses approximately $60 billion annually due to lost productivity from incarceration.
2. Increased Fiscal Burden: Governments face escalating costs associated with maintaining large prison populations. The costs of housing, feeding, and providing healthcare for inmates can strain state budgets, diverting resources away from critical areas like education and infrastructure.

To address these systemic issues, a paradigm shift in funding priorities is essential. This shift should focus on:

1. Investing in Preventive Solutions: Allocating resources to education, healthcare, and social services can help address the underlying factors that contribute to crime. By investing in communities, governments can foster environments that promote safety and well-being.

2. Reevaluating Criminal Justice Policies: Policymakers must critically assess existing criminal justice policies that prioritize incarceration. Emphasizing alternatives to

incarceration, such as restorative justice and community-based programs, can lead to better outcomes for individuals and society.

Engaging Communities in Decision-Making: Involving communities in discussions about funding priorities can lead to more effective solutions. Local input can help identify specific needs and challenges, ensuring that resources are directed to programs that have a meaningful impact.

The comparative analysis of funding allocations for prisons versus education, healthcare, and social services reveals a troubling trend: the prioritization of punitive measures over preventive solutions. This imbalance has significant implications for individuals, families, and communities, perpetuating cycles of poverty and crime while failing to address the underlying issues that contribute to criminal behavior.

To create a more equitable and effective criminal justice system, it is imperative that governments reevaluate their funding priorities. By investing in preventive solutions, communities can foster resilience and promote public safety, ultimately leading to a healthier and more just society. The time has come to shift the focus from punishment to prevention, recognizing that the true measure of a society's progress lies in its commitment to the well-being of all its members.

Chapter 4

The Ukraine Conflict: A Financial Perspective

The ongoing conflict in Ukraine has prompted significant international attention and response, particularly from the United States. This chapter delves into the financial aspects of U.S. funding to Ukraine, examining its implications for both the conflict and domestic priorities. As the U.S. government allocates billions in aid, understanding public opinion on foreign aid versus local needs is crucial to comprehending the broader impact of these financial decisions.

The roots of U.S. engagement in Ukraine can be traced back to the post-Soviet era. Following Ukraine's independence in 1991, the U.S. established a partnership aimed at promoting democracy, economic reform, and stability in the region. However, the annexation of Crimea by Russia in 2014 marked a significant turning point, prompting a more robust U.S. response, including sanctions against Russia and increased military aid to Ukraine.

The funding provided to Ukraine encompasses various forms of assistance in military, humanitarian, and economic. The U.S. government has utilized multiple mechanisms to channel funds, including the Foreign Military Financing (FMF) program, Economic Support

Fund (ESF), and direct appropriations through various legislative packages. Over the years, this funding has escalated, particularly with the onset of the full-scale invasion by Russia in February 2022.

As of late 2023, U.S. financial assistance to Ukraine has exceeded $100 billion, encompassing military support, humanitarian aid, and economic stabilization efforts. This unprecedented level of funding has raised questions about sustainability and the long-term implications for U.S. foreign policy and domestic priorities.

The allocation of vast sums to Ukraine inevitably affects domestic spending. With a finite budget, each dollar allocated abroad is a dollar not spent on domestic programs such as healthcare, education, and infrastructure. This reality has sparked debates in Congress and among the public regarding the prioritization of foreign aid versus pressing local needs.

Political factions within the U.S. exhibit varying attitudes toward foreign aid. Some advocate for robust support of Ukraine as a means to counter Russian aggression and uphold international norms, while others argue that domestic issues—such as poverty, healthcare access, and economic inequality—should take precedence. This divide is not only evident in legislative discussions but also reflects broader societal sentiments.

Public opinion on foreign aid is often mixed. Polls indicate that while there is substantial support for aiding Ukraine in the context of national security, this support diminishes when juxtaposed with domestic concerns. The perception that foreign aid diverts resources from local needs resonates with many Americans, particularly in economically challenged areas.

Proponents of U.S. funding to Ukraine argue that supporting the country is crucial for several reasons:

1. Geopolitical Stability: The conflict in Ukraine represents a broader struggle between democratic values and authoritarianism. Supporting Ukraine is seen as vital for maintaining stability in Europe and deterring further Russian aggression.

2. International Alliances: U.S. support for Ukraine reinforces relationships with NATO allies and demonstrates a commitment to collective security. This solidarity is essential for maintaining a united front against threats to democratic nations.

3. Humanitarian Responsibility: The humanitarian crisis resulting from the conflict necessitates a response. Many Americans feel a moral obligation to assist those affected by war, including millions of displaced Ukrainians.

Conversely, critics of extensive foreign aid to Ukraine emphasize the need for prioritizing domestic issues:

1. Addressing Local Challenges: With many Americans struggling with economic hardships, including inflation and job insecurity, critics argue that funds could be better spent on improving local infrastructure, education systems, and healthcare services.

2. Skepticism About Effectiveness: Some citizens question the effectiveness of foreign aid in achieving its intended outcomes. Concerns about corruption and mismanagement in recipient countries can lead to skepticism about whether U.S. taxpayer dollars are being used wisely.

3. Shifting Priorities: The focus on foreign conflicts often overshadows pressing social issues, such as homelessness, mental health crises, and systemic inequality. Advocates for these causes argue that U.S. policies should reflect the immediate needs of its citizens.

Finding a balance between funding foreign conflicts and addressing domestic priorities is a complex challenge for policymakers.

Strategies may include:

1. Targeted Aid Packages: Developing aid packages that are responsive to both international obligations and domestic needs can help reconcile these priorities. For instance, tying certain foreign aid initiatives to support for U.S. businesses or job creation could enhance public support.

2. Transparency and Accountability: Ensuring that foreign aid is allocated transparently and effectively can help

alleviate public concerns about wastefulness. Implementing rigorous oversight mechanisms can enhance trust in government spending.

3. Public Engagement: Open dialogues about the implications of foreign aid can foster a better understanding of its importance while addressing domestic needs. Engaging communities in discussions about budget priorities can help policymakers gauge public sentiment and adjust strategies accordingly.

Several instances illustrate effective balancing of domestic and foreign priorities:

1. The Marshall Plan: Post-World War II, the U.S. invested heavily in European reconstruction, which not only helped rebuild war-torn nations but also stimulated the American economy by creating markets for U.S. goods.

2. The Global Health Initiatives: Programs aimed at combating diseases such as HIV/AIDS and malaria have garnered bipartisan support. These initiatives demonstrate how foreign aid can lead to global stability while also positioning the U.S. as a leader in humanitarian efforts.

3. Disaster Relief Funding: When natural disasters occur abroad, the U.S. often mobilizes resources for relief efforts. These initiatives can bolster international goodwill and, in some cases, lead to reciprocal support during domestic crises.

4. The financial perspective of the Ukraine conflict underscores the complexities of U.S. foreign aid as it intersects with domestic priorities. As funding to Ukraine continues, the ongoing debate surrounding the balance between supporting foreign allies and addressing local needs will remain at the forefront of public discourse. Understanding the nuances of this issue is crucial for shaping effective policies that reflect both the nation's values and the priorities of its citizens. Ultimately, fostering a sustainable approach that resonates with the public can help ensure that U.S. foreign aid fulfills its intended purpose while also contributing to the welfare of Americans at home.

Chapter 5

Immigration and Funding Controversies

Immigration is a contentious issue in contemporary political discourse, often characterized by debates over funding priorities. This chapter explores how immigration funding affects local economies and communities, providing a detailed examination of funding allocations for immigration enforcement versus integration programs. Furthermore, it discusses the societal implications of these funding decisions on immigrant populations, highlighting case studies that illustrate the complex dynamics at play.

Immigration can significantly influence local economies. Immigrants often fill essential roles in various sectors, from agriculture to technology. Funding aimed at integrating immigrants into the workforce can enhance economic productivity. Programs that provide language training, vocational education, and job placement services are critical for helping immigrants transition into the labor market.

Conversely, funding focused primarily on enforcement—such as border security and detention facilities—can have adverse economic effects. Communities that rely on immigrant labor may face labor shortages if enforcement policies lead to deportations or deter new immigrants from settling. For instance, regions with significant agricultural sectors often rely on immigrant workers for seasonal labor. When enforcement funding increases, these industries may struggle to find adequate labor, resulting in lost revenue and increased prices for consumers.

California provides a compelling case study illustrating the economic ramifications of immigration funding. The state's economy heavily depends on agricultural output, which relies on a substantial immigrant workforce. A report from the California Institute for Rural Studies indicated that immigrants make up nearly 80% of the state's agricultural labor force. In recent years, increased funding for immigration enforcement has led to heightened fears among immigrant workers, causing many to avoid work during peak seasons.

In response, California has invested in integration programs, such as the California Immigrant Integration Initiative, which aims to provide resources for immigrants to participate fully in the economy. These programs have demonstrated positive outcomes in terms of economic contributions and community stability, highlighting the importance of prioritizing integration over enforcement.

The U.S. immigration system is marked by a significant disparity in funding allocation between enforcement and integration programs. The Department of Homeland Security (DHS) allocates substantial resources to immigration enforcement agencies such as Immigration and Customs Enforcement (ICE) and Customs and Border Protection (CBP). In contrast, funding for integration programs, which include community services, legal aid, and educational resources, has historically been minimal.

For example, in fiscal year 2023, the budget for ICE exceeded $8 billion, primarily for enforcement operations, while funding for the U.S. Citizenship and Immigration Services (USCIS) integration programs remained under $500 million. This stark contrast in funding reflects broader political sentiments, often driven by public fears surrounding immigration and national security.

Texas serves as another illustrative case study, showcasing the implications of prioritizing enforcement funding. The state has seen significant investment in border security measures, including the construction of barriers and increased personnel. While these efforts are framed as necessary for public safety, they have created a polarized environment, leading to tensions between immigrant communities and law enforcement.

In many Texas cities, local economies that depend on immigrant labor have expressed concerns about the impact of aggressive enforcement policies. Businesses report losing workers due to fear of detention and deportation, which in turn affects their ability to operate efficiently. This scenario has led to calls for a reevaluation of funding priorities to support integration and community safety instead of solely focusing on enforcement.

The allocation of funding for immigration policies has profound societal implications, particularly in terms of community cohesion. When funding is directed primarily toward enforcement, it can foster an atmosphere of distrust and fear among immigrant populations. This tension often spills over into the broader community, affecting relationships between immigrants and long-term residents.

Research has indicated that communities with high levels of immigration enforcement experience a decline in social cohesion. A study conducted by the American Psychological Association found that heightened enforcement leads to increased psychological stress among immigrant families, with effects on children's educational performance and overall well-being. Such findings underscore the importance of prioritizing funding that promotes integration and community building.

In contrast, funding for integration programs has demonstrated the potential to enhance social stability. Programs that offer language classes, cultural orientation, and community engagement initiatives can help immigrants adapt and thrive in their new environments. These initiatives not only benefit immigrants but also enrich the host communities by fostering diversity and intercultural understanding.

A notable example Is the Welcoming America initiative, which supports local governments in creating inclusive policies and practices for immigrants. Communities that participate in such programs often report improved relations between immigrant and non-immigrant populations, leading to greater social cohesion and mutual support.

New York City provides a robust example of the potential benefits of investing in integration programs. The city has developed a comprehensive strategy aimed at supporting immigrant communities through various initiatives, such as the NYC Immigrant Action Plan. This plan encompasses funding for legal assistance, English language courses, and job training programs.

The results have been promising. According to a report by the New York Immigrant Coalition, participants in integration programs have shown increased employment rates, higher incomes, and improved community engagement. This success illustrates how prioritizing funding for integration can yield positive outcomes, not only for immigrants but for the entire community.

The debate over immigration funding is deeply intertwined with the broader political landscape in the United States. Partisan divides often shape funding priorities, with conservative factions typically advocating for increased enforcement and liberal factions pushing for integration and support programs.

This polarization complicates the development of a cohesive immigration policy. For example, during the Trump administration, significant funding was directed toward border security and enforcement initiatives, while attempts to secure resources for integration programs faced considerable resistance. Conversely, the Biden administration has sought to balance these priorities, emphasizing the need for a more humane immigration system that supports both enforcement and integration.

In response to the divisive political climate, grassroots movements have emerged to advocate for more equitable funding practices. Organizations such as the National Immigration Forum and the American Civil Liberties Union (ACLU) have campaigned for increased investment in integration programs, highlighting their benefits for both immigrant populations and local communities.

These advocacy efforts have gained traction, resulting in some local and state governments reallocating funds to support integration initiatives. For instance, several cities have established municipal funds to assist immigrants in accessing legal services and educational resources, reflecting a growing recognition of the importance of integration in fostering community stability.

Moving forward, a critical challenge for policymakers will be to emphasize balanced funding that supports both immigration enforcement and integration.

This approach recognizes the need for national security while also addressing the realities of immigration's impact on local communities.

1. Comprehensive Review of Funding Allocation: Regular assessments of funding distribution can help identify gaps and areas needing adjustment. Allocating resources based on community needs rather than political agendas can lead to more effective outcomes.

2. Investing in Local Solutions: Encouraging local governments to devise tailored integration strategies can enhance the effectiveness of funding. By providing grants to municipalities for community-based programs, the federal government can empower local stakeholders to address specific challenges faced by immigrant populations.

3. Promoting Public Awareness: Educating the public on the benefits of integration programs is essential for garnering support. Highlighting success stories and the positive contributions of immigrants can help shift the narrative around immigration funding.

Engaging communities in the decision-making process regarding immigration funding can foster greater understanding and collaboration. Initiatives that involve immigrant voices in policy discussions can ensure that funding allocations reflect the needs and aspirations of those directly affected.

1. Community Forums and Workshops: Organizing forums that bring together immigrant communities, local businesses, and government officials can facilitate open dialogue. These discussions can serve as platforms for sharing experiences and proposing solutions.

2. Partnerships with Nonprofits: Collaborating with nonprofit organizations that work directly with immigrant populations can enhance the effectiveness of funding initiatives. Nonprofits often have valuable insights into community needs and can help facilitate the delivery of services.

The controversies surrounding immigration funding are emblematic of broader societal debates about identity, security, and community. As this chapter illustrates, the allocation of resources for immigration enforcement versus integration has profound implications for local economies and immigrant populations. By prioritizing balanced funding that promotes integration, communities can foster social cohesion, enhance economic stability, and create a more inclusive society. In navigating these complex issues, policymakers must remain attuned to the needs of all constituents, recognizing that the well-being of immigrant populations ultimately contributes to the strength and resilience of the nation as a whole.

Chapter 6

Low-Income Housing: A Forgotten Necessity

The issue of low-income housing has emerged as a critical concern in urban planning and social justice discussions. As cities grow and the inequality gap widens, the lack of sufficient affordable housing has created a crisis that not only affects individuals and families but also has far-reaching implications for entire communities. This chapter explores the complexities of the housing crisis, the role of funding in addressing these issues, the detrimental impact of insufficient low-income housing on crime rates and community wellbeing, and highlights success stories that illustrate the potential for effective funding and initiatives.

The housing crisis in the United States has reached alarming levels, with millions of families unable to secure affordable housing. According to recent statistics, approximately 11 million renters are considered "extremely low-income," spending more than 50% of their income on rent. This financial strain often leads to a cycle of poverty, where individuals are forced to choose between housing, healthcare, and other essential needs.

The crisis is exacerbated by rising property values, gentrification, and a lack of adequate government intervention. Housing prices have outpaced wage growth, leading to a situation where low-income families are increasingly pushed to the peripheries of urban areas, often resulting in longer commutes and reduced access to essential services such as education and healthcare.

The availability of funding is a pivotal factor in addressing the low-income housing crisis. Federal, state, and local government funding plays a crucial role in the development and maintenance of affordable housing. However, over the past few decades, investment in low-income housing has significantly dwindled.

Programs such as the Low-Income Housing Tax Credit (LIHTC) and Section 8 vouchers have been instrumental in providing financial support for affordable housing. The LIHTC, introduced in 1986, incentivizes private developers to create low-income housing by offering tax credits over a ten-year period. While this program has facilitated the creation of millions of affordable units, its effectiveness is often undermined by complex regulations and limited funding allocations.

Section 8 housing vouchers, which help families afford rent in the private market, have also faced increasing pressure. The demand for vouchers far exceeds supply, leaving many families without the assistance they desperately need. Moreover, funding cuts at the federal level have disproportionately affected urban areas, where the need for affordable housing is most acute.

In addition to federal programs, state and local governments have a critical role to play in funding housing initiatives. Some states have introduced their own tax credits or bonds to support affordable housing development. However, these efforts can vary significantly based on political will and economic conditions.

Community Development Block Grants (CDBG) provide additional funding for local housing initiatives, but these grants have faced cuts and restrictions, limiting their effectiveness. Local governments often struggle to balance the need for affordable housing with other pressing budgetary concerns, leading to a piecemeal approach that fails to address the scale of the crisis.

The consequences of insufficient low-income housing extend beyond mere inconvenience; they ripple throughout communities, affecting everything from public health to crime rates.

Research has demonstrated a strong correlation between housing instability and increased crime rates. Families living in unstable housing situations are often forced to relocate frequently, disrupting their social networks and support systems. This instability can lead to increased stress and anxiety, making it difficult for families to thrive.

In neighborhoods where affordable housing is scarce, residents may experience higher crime rates, not necessarily because of the residents themselves, but due to the conditions that arise from poverty and instability. Areas with limited access to quality housing often struggle with higher rates of violence and property crime, as individuals may resort to desperate measures to survive.

The lack of affordable housing also contributes to public health crises. Families living in substandard conditions are at a higher risk of exposure to health hazards such as mold, lead, and pests. Moreover, the stress associated with housing insecurity can exacerbate mental health issues, leading to a greater reliance on emergency services and healthcare systems.

Communities that lack sufficient affordable housing often have limited access to healthcare facilities and services, further compounding health disparities. For instance, low-income neighborhoods may lack pharmacies, clinics, or mental health resources, leaving residents without necessary support.

While the challenges are significant, there are numerous success stories that illustrate how effective funding and innovative approaches can successfully address the low-income housing crisis.

The LIHTC program has been a cornerstone of affordable housing development in the U.S. By providing tax incentives to developers, it has led to the creation of over three million affordable rental units since its inception. Successful projects often integrate supportive services, such as job training and education programs, which help residents achieve economic stability.

One notable example is the redevelopment of the former Pruitt-Igoe housing project in St. Louis, Missouri. Once a symbol of urban decay, the area has been transformed into a vibrant community with a mix of affordable housing, parks, and community spaces, made possible through LIHTC funding and community engagement.

Community land trusts (CLTs) represent another innovative model for promoting affordable housing. CLTs are nonprofit organizations that acquire land to develop affordable housing while ensuring long-term affordability for residents. By removing land from the speculative real estate market, CLTs can stabilize neighborhoods and provide secure housing options.

One successful example is the Champlain Housing Trust in Burlington, Vermont, which has developed over 2,000 affordable housing units. The trust allows residents to purchase homes while retaining long-term affordability through shared equity models, ensuring that homes remain accessible to low-income families.

Inclusionary zoning policies require developers to include a percentage of affordable units in new housing developments. This approach has been successfully implemented in cities like San Francisco and New York City, where the need for affordable housing is particularly acute. By leveraging the private sector's involvement in addressing housing shortages, inclusionary zoning can provide a steady stream of affordable units without relying solely on public funding.

The low-income housing crisis is a multifaceted issue that requires comprehensive solutions, including increased funding, innovative policy approaches, and community engagement. The connection between housing, crime, and public health underscores the urgent need for action. Success stories from across the nation demonstrate that with the right commitment and resources, it is possible to create effective housing solutions that not only provide shelter but also foster community stability and wellbeing.

As we move forward, it is crucial for policymakers, community leaders, and advocates to prioritize low-income housing as a fundamental necessity, recognizing that the wellbeing of our communities depends on it. By investing in affordable housing initiatives, we can pave the way for healthier, safer, and more equitable communities for all.

Chapter 7

The Cycle of Poverty and Crime

The intricate relationship between poverty and crime is a perennial issue that has long captivated the attention of researchers, policymakers, and social activists. This chapter delves into the dynamics of how poverty can lead to increased crime rates and the role inadequate funding for social services plays in perpetuating this cycle. Additionally, we will explore case studies of successful intervention programs that have addressed these issues, demonstrating that targeted funding and comprehensive social services can break the cycle of poverty and crime.

The cycle of poverty and crime is marked by a complex interplay of socioeconomic factors. Individuals living in poverty often face a multitude of challenges, including limited access to education, healthcare, and employment opportunities. This lack of resources can lead to desperation and a higher likelihood of engaging in criminal activity as a means of survival.

Research has shown that neighborhoods with high poverty rates tend to experience higher crime rates. For instance, a study from the National Institute of Justice found that areas with concentrated poverty are more likely to experience violent crime. This correlation can be attributed to several factors, including social disorganization, lack of community cohesion, and limited access to law enforcement and social services.

Inadequate funding for social services exacerbates the challenges faced by those living in poverty. When essential services such as mental health care, substance abuse treatment, and educational programs are underfunded, individuals and families are left without the support they need to escape poverty. This lack of support can lead to increased stress, mental health issues, and ultimately, a higher propensity for criminal behavior.

Funding cuts to social services often lead to a reliance on the criminal justice system as a means of addressing social issues. For example, individuals with untreated mental health issues may find themselves in conflict with the law, leading to arrest and incarceration rather than receiving the help they need. This reliance on punitive measures rather than preventative and rehabilitative services contributes to the cycle of poverty and crime.

Education is one of the most powerful tools for breaking the cycle of poverty. However, inadequate funding for schools in low-income areas often results in overcrowded classrooms, outdated materials, and a lack of extracurricular programs. Students in these environments may feel disengaged and unsupported, leading to higher dropout rates.

The link between education and crime is well-documented. Young people who drop out of school are at a significantly higher risk of becoming involved in criminal activity. A study by the Bureau of Justice Statistics found that individuals without a high school diploma are more likely to be incarcerated than those with higher levels of education. By failing to invest in education, society inadvertently perpetuates

Mental health issues and substance abuse are prevalent among individuals living in poverty, yet access to treatment is often severely limited due to funding constraints. Many low-income individuals lack health insurance or the means to pay for necessary services, leading to untreated conditions that can result in criminal behavior.

For example, individuals with untreated mental health disorders may engage in criminal activity due to impaired judgment or a lack of coping mechanisms. Additionally, substance abuse is frequently linked to criminal behavior, as individuals may resort to theft or drug-related offenses to support their addiction. Without adequate funding for mental health and substance abuse treatment, these issues remain unaddressed, further entrenching individuals in the cycle of poverty and crime.

As social services become underfunded, the criminal justice system often becomes the default response to social issues. Instead of addressing the root causes of crime, such as poverty and lack of support, society tends to rely on punitive measures. This overreliance not only fails to resolve the underlying issues but also leads to the criminalization of poverty.

Incarceration has become a common outcome for individuals who engage in criminal behavior as a result of socioeconomic factors. The costs associated with incarceration are staggering, both for individuals and society as a whole. Incarcerated individuals often face significant barriers to reintegration upon release, including job loss, disrupted family connections, and diminished access to social services. This cycle of incarceration creates a revolving door effect, where individuals are repeatedly trapped in the system, unable to escape the cycle of poverty and crime.

While the challenges are significant, there are numerous intervention programs that have successfully addressed the relationship between poverty, crime, and funding. These programs demonstrate that with the right resources and support, it is possible to break the cycle of poverty and crime.

The Cure Violence program, launched in Chicago, Illinois, takes an innovative public health approach to reducing violence. The program treats violence as an infectious disease, aiming to interrupt and prevent its spread through community engagement, conflict mediation, and outreach.

Cure Violence employs "violence interrupters," who are individuals from the community trained to mediate conflicts before they escalate into violent acts. By focusing on high-risk individuals and areas, the program has seen significant reductions in gun violence. For instance, a study conducted by the University of Chicago found that neighborhoods with Cure Violence programs experienced a 43% reduction in shootings.

The success of Cure Violence highlights the importance of funding for community-driven initiatives that address the root causes of violence. By investing in outreach and mediation rather than punitive measures, cities can create safer environments and break the cycle of violence and poverty.

The Harlem Children's Zone (HCZ) in New York City is a comprehensive community initiative aimed at combating poverty through education and social services. The HCZ model provides a wide range of services, including early childhood education, after-school programs, health services, and college support for families living in poverty.

One of the key components of the HCZ is its focus on creating a "cradle-to-college" pipeline, ensuring that children receive the support they need at every stage of their development. The program has demonstrated significant improvements in educational outcomes, with students in the HCZ outperforming their peers in nearby schools.

By addressing the multifaceted challenges faced by families living in poverty, the Harlem Children's Zone exemplifies how targeted funding for education and social services can break the cycle of poverty and crime. The success of the HCZ model has inspired similar initiatives across the country, highlighting the potential for comprehensive approaches to address poverty and its associated challenges.

The Boston Reentry Initiative (BRI) is a collaborative program aimed at supporting individuals returning from incarceration. Recognizing that successful reintegration is crucial for reducing recidivism, the BRI provides a range of services, including job training, housing assistance, and mental health support.

The program emphasizes the importance of building partnerships between law enforcement, social services, and community organizations. By fostering collaboration, the BRI helps individuals navigate the challenges of reentry, addressing the root causes of criminal behavior and promoting stability.

Evidence suggests that the BRI has led to significant reductions in recidivism rates among participants. A study conducted by the Boston Foundation found that individuals who engaged with the BRI were 30% less likely to be re-arrested than those who did not participate. These findings underscore the importance of investing in reentry programs that address the needs of individuals returning to their communities.

The cycle of poverty and crime is a complex issue that requires a multifaceted response. Inadequate funding for social services perpetuates this cycle, leading to increased crime rates and reliance on the criminal justice system. However, as demonstrated by successful intervention programs, it is possible to break this cycle through targeted funding and comprehensive support.

Programs like Cure Violence, the Harlem Children's Zone, and the Boston Reentry Initiative illustrate the impact of investing in community-driven solutions that address the root causes of poverty and crime. By prioritizing funding for education, mental health services, and reentry support, society can create pathways for individuals to escape poverty and build safer, more stable communities.

As we move forward, it is crucial for policymakers, community leaders, and advocates to recognize the interconnectedness of poverty and crime and to support funding initiatives that promote social services. By doing so, we can work toward breaking the cycle of poverty and crime, fostering a healthier and more equitable society for all.

Chapter 8

The Role of Advocacy and Activism

In recent years, grassroots movements have emerged as powerful forces in advocating for the reallocation of public funds towards more equitable and just initiatives. These movements often arise from community members who are directly affected by funding decisions, representing a diverse range of issues including education, healthcare, housing, environmental justice, and social services. The underlying principle of these movements is to challenge existing power structures and demand that resources be directed towards communities that have historically been marginalized or underfunded.

Grassroots advocacy often begins at the local level, where residents identify pressing needs that are not being adequately addressed by government budgets. For example, communities facing high levels of poverty may call for increased funding for public schools, affordable housing, or mental health services. Organizers leverage their personal experiences and collective narratives to highlight the disparities faced by their communities, drawing attention to the inequities in resource allocation.

These movements utilize a variety of strategies to amplify their voices. Social media campaigns, public demonstrations, and community forums serve as platforms for raising awareness and mobilizing support. By harnessing the power of storytelling, grassroots advocates can connect with broader audiences and foster empathy for their causes. This narrative approach is particularly effective in humanizing the issues at stake, making it easier for potential allies to understand the real-world implications of funding decisions.

Additionally, grassroots movements often collaborate with established organizations, such as non-profits and advocacy groups, to enhance their impact. These partnerships can provide access to resources, expertise, and networks that are essential for effective advocacy. Together, they can conduct research, develop policy proposals, and engage in lobbying efforts to influence decision-makers.

The power of grassroots advocacy is best illustrated through success stories that have resulted in tangible changes to funding priorities. One notable example is the movement for increased funding for public education in the United States. In several states, teachers and parents have organized protests and strikes, demanding fair wages for educators and adequate resources for schools. These efforts have led to significant policy changes, including increased funding allocations and the implementation of more equitable funding formulas.

In Chicago, the "Raise Your Hand" coalition emerged in response to deep cuts to public school funding. Through persistent advocacy, community members successfully pressured local officials to allocate additional resources towards underfunded schools. Their efforts not only resulted in increased funding but also fostered a more inclusive decision-making process that allowed parents and educators to have a say in how funds were spent.

Another compelling example comes from the environmental justice movement. Communities of color, often disproportionately affected by pollution and environmental degradation, have organized to demand that local governments prioritize environmental health in their funding decisions. In Richmond, California, residents successfully advocated for the establishment of a community-based environmental health program, which redirected funds towards monitoring air quality and addressing the health impacts of industrial pollution.

These examples illustrate how grassroots advocacy can lead to meaningful changes in funding priorities. By mobilizing community members, raising public awareness, and engaging with policymakers, these movements have demonstrated that collective action can challenge entrenched systems and create a more equitable distribution of resources.

Public engagement and awareness are critical components of any successful advocacy campaign. Without a broad base of support, grassroots movements may struggle to gain traction or influence decision-makers. Engaging the public not only builds momentum but also educates individuals about the issues at stake, fostering a sense of shared responsibility and collective action.

One effective strategy for increasing public engagement is through educational initiatives. Workshops, informational sessions, and community meetings can empower residents with knowledge about the funding processes and the specific issues affecting their communities. This education can demystify complex budgetary decisions and encourage individuals to voice their concerns and participate in advocacy efforts.

Social media has also transformed the landscape of public engagement. Platforms like Twitter, Facebook, and Instagram allow grassroots movements to reach wider audiences quickly and effectively. Campaigns can go viral, drawing attention to specific issues and mobilizing support from individuals who may not be directly affected but are sympathetic to the cause. Hashtags and online petitions can amplify messages and create a sense of urgency around funding reallocations.

Moreover, public demonstrations serve as powerful visual statements of solidarity and urgency. Events such as marches, rallies, and sit-ins can capture media attention and generate public discourse, bringing issues to the forefront of community and political conversations. When people see large groups advocating for change, it can inspire others to join the movement and lend their voices to the cause.

Engaging with local media is another crucial aspect of building public awareness. Grassroots advocates can cultivate relationships with journalists to ensure that their stories and perspectives are represented. By sharing personal narratives and data-driven research, advocates can paint a comprehensive picture of the challenges they face and the solutions they propose. This media coverage can help legitimize their efforts and put pressure on decision-makers to respond to public demands.

Ultimately, public engagement is about creating a sense of community ownership over the issues at hand. When individuals feel personally invested in the outcomes, they are more likely to act, whether that means attending a meeting, contacting their representatives, or participating in protests. By fostering a culture of engagement, grassroots movements can build the collective power necessary to effect change.

The role of advocacy and activism in reallocating funds is a testament to the power of grassroots movements to effect change. Through community organizing, storytelling, and strategic partnerships, these movements have successfully challenged inequitable funding practices and brought about significant policy changes. The importance of public engagement and awareness cannot be overstated; they are essential to building the momentum needed for sustained advocacy efforts.

As we look to the future, it is clear that grassroots movements will continue to play a vital role in shaping funding priorities and addressing systemic inequities. By amplifying the voices of those most affected by funding decisions, these movements not only advocate for change but also empower communities to reclaim their agency. The journey toward a more equitable distribution of resources is ongoing, but with continued advocacy and public engagement, there is hope for a future where funding priorities reflect the needs and aspirations of all communities.

Chapter 9

Policy Solutions and Innovations

In the face of persistent social issues, innovative funding solutions are essential for driving change and improving community well-being. Traditional funding models often fail to address the complexities of social problems, leading to a cycle of ineffective responses. To break this cycle, policymakers and advocates are exploring new approaches that prioritize long-term solutions over short-term fixes. This chapter examines some of these innovative funding solutions, highlighting their potential to transform social service delivery.

One innovative approach gaining traction is the use of social impact bonds (SIBs). SIBs are a form of pay-for-success financing in which private investors fund social programs upfront, with the government reimbursing them only if the programs meet specific outcomes. This model aligns financial incentives with social outcomes, encouraging efficiency and effectiveness in service delivery.

For example, the Massachusetts Juvenile Justice Pay for Success Initiative aimed to reduce recidivism among young offenders. Investors funded a program providing intensive mentoring and support services to at-risk youth. If the program successfully reduced reoffending rates, the state would repay investors with interest. This approach not only mobilizes private capital but also emphasizes accountability and measurable outcomes, allowing for data-driven decision-making.

Another innovative funding solution is the collective impact framework, which brings together diverse stakeholders—government agencies, non-profits, businesses, and community members—to address complex social issues collaboratively. This model emphasizes shared goals, aligned efforts, and continuous communication to create systemic change.

In the case of early childhood education, collective impact initiatives have emerged in various communities to improve educational outcomes for young children. By pooling resources and coordinating efforts, stakeholders can implement comprehensive strategies that address multiple facets of child development. Funding can be allocated more effectively when stakeholders work together, leading to better outcomes for children and families.

Crowdfunding has also emerged as a novel way to finance social initiatives. Online platforms allow individuals and organizations to raise small amounts of money from a large number of people, democratizing the funding process. This approach empowers communities to take control of their funding needs, often bypassing traditional funding sources that may be slow or restrictive.

For instance, grassroots organizations have successfully used crowdfunding to support local projects, from community gardens to youth programs. By engaging the community in fundraising efforts, these initiatives foster a sense of ownership and investment in the outcomes. Moreover, crowdfunding campaigns often use social media to amplify their reach, raising awareness and mobilizing support beyond local boundaries.

Flexible funding models are another promising approach to addressing social issues. Traditional funding often comes with strict guidelines and limited flexibility, making it difficult for organizations to adapt to changing needs. Flexible funding allows organizations to allocate resources where they are most needed, fostering innovation and responsiveness.

For example, in the realm of mental health services, some funders are beginning to adopt flexible funding practices that enable organizations to experiment with new service delivery models. This adaptability can lead to the development of more effective interventions that meet the unique needs of diverse populations.

The shift from punitive measures to rehabilitation-focused policies has gained momentum in recent years, reflecting a growing recognition of the need for more humane and effective approaches to criminal justice. Several successful policy changes illustrate this trend, demonstrating the potential for transformative impact on individuals and communities.

One of the most significant movements towards rehabilitation is the broader criminal justice reform movement, which advocates for policies that prioritize rehabilitation over incarceration. Many jurisdictions are reevaluating their sentencing practices, particularly for non-violent offenses. For instance, several states have implemented policies that reduce mandatory minimum sentences, allowing judges more discretion in sentencing. This flexibility enables judges to consider individual circumstances and opt for rehabilitation programs instead of incarceration.

Drug courts are another successful example of policy changes that prioritize rehabilitation. These specialized courts focus on providing treatment and support for individuals with substance use disorders rather than subjecting them to traditional criminal justice processes. Participants in drug courts are required to undergo treatment, regular drug testing, and frequent court appearances, but they can avoid incarceration if they comply with the program's requirements.

Research has shown that drug courts can significantly reduce recidivism rates and improve overall outcomes for participants. By addressing the underlying issues of addiction, these programs not only help individuals regain control of their lives but also reduce the burden on the criminal justice system.

Communities across the country are also exploring community-based alternatives to incarceration. Initiatives such as restorative justice programs emphasize healing and accountability rather than punishment. These programs bring together victims, offenders, and community members to discuss the impact of the crime and collaboratively determine a path forward. This approach fosters understanding, reconciliation, and a sense of community responsibility.

For example, in Washington State, the "Community Accountability Program" allows individuals charged with low-level offenses to participate in restorative justice processes instead of going through the traditional court system. Participants complete community service, engage in dialogue with victims, and take steps to repair the harm caused by their actions. This model not only reduces incarceration rates but also encourages personal accountability and community healing.

Several states have enacted legislative reforms aimed at reducing the reliance on incarceration. For instance, California's Proposition 47, passed in 2014, reclassified certain non-violent felonies as misdemeanors, leading to the release of thousands of individuals from prison. The initiative also redirected funds saved from reduced incarceration costs to support mental health and substance abuse treatment programs, underscoring the potential for policy changes to create a more equitable system.

Similarly, New York's "Raise the Age" legislation, implemented in 2018, raised the age of criminal responsibility from 16 to 18. This significant change reflects a growing understanding that adolescents are fundamentally different from adults in terms of development and decision-making. By treating young offenders within a rehabilitative framework, the state aims to reduce recidivism and promote positive life outcomes.

Preventive measures play a crucial role in addressing social issues before they escalate into more significant problems. Shifting funding towards prevention is not only cost-effective but also promotes healthier, more resilient communities. This section discusses the potential for funding innovations that prioritize preventive measures across various sectors.

One of the most impactful areas for preventive funding is early childhood development. Research consistently shows that investments in early education and supportive services yield significant long-term benefits, including improved academic performance, better health outcomes, and reduced criminal behavior. By reallocating funds towards early childhood programs, communities can address disparities before they become entrenched.

Programs such as home visiting services, preschool education, and parental support initiatives have demonstrated success in enhancing child development and family stability. For instance, the Nurse-Family Partnership program, which provides home visits from nurses to low-income first-time mothers, has shown significant improvements in maternal and child health, as well as reduced involvement with the criminal justice system.

Community-based prevention programs offer another avenue for shifting funding towards proactive measures. Programs that focus on youth engagement, mentorship, and skill-building can divert young people from pathways leading to crime or substance abuse. For example, after-school programs that provide safe spaces for youth to engage in constructive activities have been shown to reduce delinquency rates.

Funding these programs not only helps prevent negative outcomes but also fosters community cohesion and resilience. By investing in youth development, communities can create environments that support positive behavior and reduce the need for punitive interventions later on.

The public health sector has increasingly recognized the importance of preventive measures in addressing social issues. By shifting funding towards preventive health initiatives, communities can tackle the root causes of problems such as addiction, mental health crises, and chronic disease.

For instance, investing in mental health awareness campaigns and access to mental health services can prevent crises that often lead to interactions with law enforcement. Similarly, funding addiction prevention programs can reduce the prevalence of substance use disorders, ultimately decreasing the burden on the criminal justice system and healthcare services.

Implementing preventive measures often requires collaboration across various sectors, including education, health, and social services. Collaborative funding strategies can facilitate this integration, allowing stakeholders to pool resources and share expertise. For example, public-private partnerships can leverage funding from both government and private sectors to support comprehensive prevention initiatives.

These partnerships can also foster innovation by encouraging organizations to work together to develop and implement evidence-based practices that address complex social issues. By aligning funding with shared goals, stakeholders can create sustainable solutions that benefit the entire community.

Conclusion

Innovative funding solutions and policy changes have the potential to transform the landscape of social issues, shifting the focus from punitive measures to rehabilitation and prevention. By exploring new funding models such as social impact bonds, collective impact frameworks, and flexible funding, communities can develop more effective and responsive strategies to address complex challenges.

Successful examples of rehabilitation-focused policies demonstrate the effectiveness of prioritizing support and services over incarceration. By investing in preventive measures, communities can create healthier, more resilient environments that address the root causes of social issues before they escalate.

As we move forward, it is crucial to continue advocating for funding innovations and policy changes that prioritize rehabilitation and prevention. By doing so, we can foster a more equitable and just society, ultimately improving outcomes for individuals and communities alike.

Chapter 10

The Politics of Funding

Funding decisions in public policy and governance are rarely made in a vacuum. They are deeply intertwined with the political landscape, shaped by a myriad of factors including partisanship, lobbying efforts, and the interests of special groups. Understanding the politics of funding is crucial for comprehending how resources are allocated, which projects receive support, and ultimately, how public policy is shaped and implemented. In this chapter, we will delve into the political motivations behind funding decisions, explore the influence of partisanship, and examine the critical role of lobbyists and special interests.

The Political Motivations Behind Funding Decisions

At the core of funding decisions lies a complex web of political motivations. Politicians and policymakers are often driven by a desire to secure votes, satisfy constituents, and fulfill campaign promises. These motivations can lead to funding allocations that prioritize certain projects over others, often reflecting the political landscape rather than the actual needs of the community.

Voter Influence and Constituency Needs

Politicians are acutely aware of the needs and preferences of their constituents. Funding decisions can be influenced by the desire to gain favor with voters. For example, a legislator may advocate for funding for a new highway or school in their district, not only because it serves a public need but also because it enhances their visibility and popularity among voters. This phenomenon is particularly evident during election cycles, when funding announcements can be strategically timed to maximize electoral benefit.

Ideological Alignment

Political ideologies play a significant role in shaping funding priorities. Different parties have distinct views on the role of government and the allocation of resources. For instance, conservative lawmakers may prioritize funding for defense and law enforcement, while liberal lawmakers may focus on social services and environmental initiatives. This ideological divide can lead to significant disparities in funding allocation, often resulting in contentious debates over budget proposals.

Partisanship and Resource Allocation

Partisanship significantly influences how resources are allocated at both the federal and state levels. The increasing polarization of American politics means that funding decisions are often viewed through a partisan lens, with parties vying for control over budgets and resources.

The Budget Process

The budget process is a critical arena where partisanship manifests. Each year, the executive branch proposes a budget, which is then subject to negotiation and modification by the legislative branch. In a divided government, where one party controls the presidency and the other controls one or both chambers of Congress, partisan conflicts can lead to gridlock and delayed funding.

During negotiations, party leaders may leverage funding as a bargaining chip to secure support for their priorities. This can result in compromises that dilute funding for programs favored by one party in exchange for concessions on other issues. Moreover, the creation of earmarks—funds allocated for specific projects—can be used to garner bipartisan support, though this practice has also faced significant criticism for fostering waste and inefficiency.

Partisan Disparities in Funding

Research has shown that partisan control can lead to disparities in funding allocation. For instance, during periods of unified government, parties may be more successful in directing resources to their preferred programs. Conversely, in a divided government, funding may be distributed more evenly across party lines as a means of compromise, which can dilute the effectiveness of targeted funding initiatives.

The Role of Lobbyists and Special Interests

Lobbyists and special interest groups play a pivotal role in shaping funding priorities. These entities often have significant resources and expertise, allowing them to influence policymakers and sway funding decisions in their favor.

The Mechanics of Lobbying

Lobbying involves advocating for specific interests, often through direct contact with legislators and government officials. Lobbyists use various tactics, including providing research, drafting legislation, and mobilizing grassroots campaigns, to persuade policymakers to allocate funds to particular causes. This can lead to an uneven playing field where well-funded interests dominate the conversation, overshadowing the needs of less influential groups.

Case Studies of Lobbying Influence

Several case studies illustrate the impact of lobbying on funding decisions. For example, the pharmaceutical industry spends billions on lobbying efforts to influence healthcare policy and funding for drug research. These efforts often result in favorable legislation that prioritizes pharmaceutical interests, sometimes at the expense of public health initiatives.

Similarly, environmental groups lobby for funding to combat climate change, advocating for renewable energy projects and conservation efforts. While their influence can lead to positive outcomes for the environment, it also highlights the competition among various interests vying for limited resources.

The Ethical Considerations of Lobbying

The influence of lobbyists raises ethical questions about the integrity of the funding process. Critics argue that excessive lobbying can lead to corruption and a lack of accountability, as special interests may prioritize their agendas over the public good. Transparency in lobbying activities is essential to ensure that funding decisions reflect the needs of the community rather than the interests of a select few.

Conclusion

The politics of funding is a complex interplay of motivations, ideologies, and influences. Understanding the political landscape is crucial for grasping how resources are allocated, and which projects receive support. Partisanship shapes funding decisions, often leading to disparities based on political affiliation. Additionally, lobbyists and special interest groups exert significant influence, raising ethical considerations about the fairness and transparency of the funding process.

To ensure that funding decisions serve the public interest, it is essential to promote greater transparency in lobbying, encourage bipartisan cooperation, and prioritize the needs of constituents over political agendas. As the political landscape continues to evolve, the dynamics of funding will remain a critical area of study for policymakers, researchers, and citizens alike.

Chapter 11

Future Generations: Investing Wisely

The decisions made today regarding funding allocation have profound implications for future generations. As policymakers grapple with immediate needs and political pressures, the long-term consequences of these choices can often be overlooked. This chapter examines the importance of investing wisely in key areas such as education, mental health, and community services, and discusses the potential future scenarios if current funding trends continue. By analyzing the implications of present funding decisions, we can better understand how to build a more sustainable and equitable future.

The Long-Term Impact of Current Funding Decisions

Funding decisions are not merely financial transactions; they are investments in the future of society. The allocation of resources today shapes the landscape of tomorrow, influencing everything from economic stability to social cohesion. Understanding this long-term impact is essential for responsible governance.

Economic Consequences

Investments in critical areas such as education and infrastructure can yield significant economic returns. For instance, funding education not only equips individuals with the skills needed for the workforce but also fosters innovation and productivity. Conversely, underfunding education can lead to a less skilled workforce, reduced economic growth, and increased reliance on social services.

In addition to education, infrastructure investments—such as public transportation, roads, and digital connectivity—are vital for economic development. Poor infrastructure can stifle business growth and deter investment, leading to long-term economic stagnation. Therefore, decisions made today regarding these funding areas will resonate through the economy for generations to come.

The social fabric of communities is also shaped by funding decisions. Investments in mental health services and community programs play a crucial role in promoting well-being and social stability. When governments prioritize these services, they contribute to healthier, more resilient communities.

On the other hand, neglecting these areas can lead to a host of societal problems, including increased crime rates, homelessness, and social disconnection. Such issues not only impose immediate costs on society but also create long-term challenges that can burden future generations. The social implications of funding decisions underscore the need for a holistic approach to resource allocation.

Education is one of the most critical areas for investment, with long-lasting effects on individuals and society as a whole. It empowers individuals, drives economic growth, and fosters social equality. However, the current funding landscape for education often reflects disparities that need to be addressed.

Education serves as a powerful tool for economic mobility. Access to quality education can break the cycle of poverty, providing individuals with the skills and knowledge needed to secure well-paying jobs. Investments in early childhood education, K-12 programs, and higher education are essential for creating pathways to opportunity.

Research has consistently shown that children who receive quality education are more likely to succeed academically and professionally. Conversely, those who are denied access to educational opportunities face significant barriers that can perpetuate cycles of disadvantage. For future generations, prioritizing education funding is not just a moral imperative; it is an economic necessity.

Unfortunately, disparities in education funding often mirror broader social inequalities. Schools in affluent areas tend to receive more resources than those in low-income communities, leading to unequal educational outcomes. Investing in education must involve a commitment to equity, ensuring that all children—regardless of their background—have access to quality education.

Efforts to address these disparities can include increasing funding for under-resourced schools, expanding access to early childhood education, and implementing policies that promote equitable distribution of resources. By investing wisely in education, we can create a more just society and foster opportunities for all future generations.

Mental health is a critical component of overall well-being, yet it remains an area that is frequently underfunded. The stigma surrounding mental health issues often leads to neglect in policy discussions, despite the significant impact mental health has on individuals and society.

Mental health disorders affect millions of individuals, and their repercussions extend beyond the individual to families, communities, and the economy. Untreated mental health issues can lead to increased healthcare costs, loss of productivity, and social instability. Conversely, investing in mental health services can yield substantial benefits, including improved quality of life, reduced healthcare costs, and enhanced community cohesion.

For future generations, addressing mental health funding is crucial. As awareness of mental health issues grows, the demand for services is likely to increase. Policymakers must ensure that mental health services are adequately funded and accessible to all, particularly in schools and community settings.

A holistic approach to health funding should integrate mental health into broader health initiatives. This can involve training primary care providers to recognize and address mental health issues, increasing funding for community-based mental health programs, and promoting mental health education in schools.

Investing in mental health is not just a response to current needs; it is an investment in the future resilience of society. By prioritizing mental health, we can foster healthier individuals and communities, ultimately benefiting future generations.

Community services play a vital role in enhancing the quality of life for individuals and families. These services encompass a wide range of programs, including housing assistance, food security initiatives, and social services.

Community services are essential for addressing immediate needs and fostering long-term stability. They provide crucial support to vulnerable populations, helping individuals navigate challenges such as unemployment, health crises, and family instability. By investing in community services, governments can create a safety net that prevents individuals from falling into poverty and despair.

Moreover, community services promote social cohesion by fostering connections among individuals and groups. Programs that encourage community engagement and volunteerism can strengthen social bonds, creating resilient communities that support one another in times of need.

Neglecting community services can have dire consequences. When funding is cut, vulnerable populations often bear the brunt of these decisions, leading to increased hardship and social dislocation. For future generations, the underfunding of community services can create a cycle of disadvantages, making it more difficult for individuals to escape poverty and achieve stability.

Investing in community services is not simply a matter of charity; it is a strategic approach to building a healthier, more equitable society. As we look to the future, prioritizing these services will be essential for ensuring that all individuals have the support they need to thrive.

If current funding trends persist, the implications for future generations could be grim. A lack of investment in education, mental health, and community services may lead to a host of challenges that will be difficult to overcome.

Continued underinvestment in education and infrastructure could result in an increasingly unskilled workforce, stifling economic growth. As technology evolves and the job market shifts, individuals who lack the necessary skills will find it increasingly difficult to compete. This economic stagnation could lead to higher unemployment rates and greater income inequality, ultimately burdening future generations with economic challenges.

The consequences of neglecting mental health and community services could manifest in rising rates of mental health disorders, homelessness, and social unrest. As communities become more fragmented and support systems erode, individuals may find themselves isolated and struggling to cope with life's challenges. This social disconnection can lead to increased crime rates, reduced civic engagement, and a decline in overall quality of life.

If funding disparities persist, the gap between affluent and disadvantaged communities is likely to widen. Children from low-income families will continue to face barriers to education and opportunity, perpetuating cycles of poverty. The long-term effects of this inequality can be devastating, leading to a society where a small percentage of individuals thrive while the majority struggle to make ends meet.

Investing wisely in education, mental health, and community services is essential for securing a better future for generations to come. The long-term impact of current funding decisions cannot be overstated; they shape the social, economic, and health landscapes of tomorrow. By prioritizing these critical areas, we can create a more equitable and resilient society that empowers individuals and fosters community well-being.

As we move forward, it is crucial for policymakers, community leaders, and citizens to advocate for responsible funding decisions that reflect the needs of all members of society. The choices we make today will resonate far into the future, and investing wisely is the key to building a brighter tomorrow for generations yet to come.

Chapter 12

Reimagining the Funding Framework

In contemporary society, the challenges we face—ranging from climate change and public health crises to social injustice—are complex and interconnected. Traditional funding frameworks often fall short of addressing these multifaceted issues. This chapter proposes a holistic approach to funding societal problems, emphasizing the necessity for interdisciplinary collaboration, innovative funding strategies, and the creation of more equitable models. By reimagining how we allocate resources, we can foster sustainable solutions that benefit all segments of society.

A holistic funding framework recognizes the intricate web of factors contributing to societal challenges. For instance, addressing poverty cannot be achieved solely through financial aid; it requires a comprehensive strategy that includes education, healthcare, and employment opportunities.

Modern problems are rarely isolated. Climate change impacts public health, economic stability, and social equity. Therefore, funding strategies must reflect this interconnectedness. A holistic approach encourages funders to look beyond traditional silos, fostering a systems-thinking mindset that considers how various elements interact.

The COVID-19 pandemic starkly illustrated the need for holistic funding. The health crisis was not just a medical issue; it had profound implications for the economy, mental health, and social systems. Countries that adopted a comprehensive response—integrating healthcare, economic support, and mental health services—were more effective in mitigating the pandemic's effects. This experience underscores the importance of funding models that support integrated solutions.

To create effective funding frameworks, interdisciplinary collaboration is essential. This collaboration involves stakeholders from various sectors, including government, non-profits, academia, and the private sector. Each entity brings unique insights, resources, and expertise, paving the way for innovative solutions.

Creating partnerships among diverse organizations can enhance the effectiveness of funding initiatives. For example, a collaboration between a healthcare provider and a local educational institution can lead to programs that address health literacy, ultimately improving community health outcomes.

Often, there is a disconnect between the sectors that address social issues. Nonprofits may focus on immediate needs, while government agencies might prioritize long-term strategies. Bridging this gap requires open communication and shared objectives. Funders can play a crucial role in facilitating these dialogues, ensuring that diverse perspectives are integrated into funding decisions.

Interdisciplinary collaboration fosters innovation. When experts from different fields come together, they can develop creative solutions that a single discipline might overlook. For instance, combining insights from urban planning and public health can lead to the design of cities that promote well-being, reduce pollution, and enhance social cohesion.

Equity must be at the forefront of any reimagined funding framework. Traditional funding models often perpetuate disparities, leaving marginalized communities underserved. To create a more equitable model, we must re-evaluate how funds are allocated and who gets to decide.

One strategy for achieving equity in funding is to prioritize underrepresented communities. This can involve targeting resources toward initiatives that directly benefit marginalized groups, ensuring that their voices are heard in the decision-making process.

Empowering communities to lead initiatives can significantly enhance funding effectiveness. When communities have a say in how resources are allocated, they are more likely to create solutions that reflect their needs. Funders can support this by providing flexible funding that allows communities to innovate and adapt their approaches.

Decentralizing decision-making power is another crucial element of equitable funding. Traditional funding models often concentrate power in a few entities, which can lead to biases and inequitable outcomes. By involving a broader range of stakeholders in the decision-making process, we can ensure that diverse perspectives are considered.

Data can be a powerful tool in creating equitable funding models. By leveraging technology and data analytics, funders can identify gaps in funding distribution and track the impact of their investments. This transparency can help hold funders accountable and ensure that resources are directed where they are most needed.

To support a holistic and equitable approach to funding, we must explore innovative funding mechanisms. These mechanisms can provide the flexibility and creativity necessary to tackle complex societal issues.

Social impact bonds (SIBs) are a promising model that aligns financial incentives with social outcomes. In this model, private investors provide upfront capital for social programs, and the government repays them based on the success of those programs. This approach encourages innovation and accountability, as investors are motivated to support effective solutions.

Crowdfunding platforms enable individuals and communities to raise funds for specific projects. This democratizes funding and allows grassroots initiatives to thrive. Community financing models, such as cooperatives, also empower local residents to invest in their projects, fostering a sense of ownership and commitment.

Blended finance combines public and private funding sources to address social issues. By leveraging private investment alongside public funds, we can achieve greater scale and impact. This approach is particularly effective in sectors like renewable energy, where upfront costs can be prohibitive.

Adaptive funding models allow for flexibility in project implementation. These models recognize that social issues are dynamic and can change over time. Funders can provide resources that adapt to evolving needs, ensuring that initiatives remain relevant and effective.

Reimagining the funding framework is essential for addressing the complex societal issues we face today. A holistic approach that emphasizes interdisciplinary collaboration, equity, and innovative funding mechanisms can create sustainable solutions that benefit all members of society. By prioritizing underrepresented communities, decentralizing decision-making, and embracing new funding models, we can build a more just and equitable future. As we move forward, it is imperative that funders, policymakers, and community leaders work together to implement these strategies, fostering a collaborative environment that drives meaningful change.

Chapter 13

Global Perspectives on Funding

In an increasingly interconnected world, examining how different countries approach funding for societal issues can provide invaluable insights and lessons. Diverse funding models, tailored to specific cultural, economic, and political contexts, reveal innovative practices that can inform U.S. policy. This chapter explores global perspectives on funding, focusing on how various nations tackle similar issues, the lessons learned from these international models, and the potential implications for funding strategies in the United States. Global Approaches to Funding

Scandinavia: The Nordic Model

Countries such as Sweden, Norway, and Denmark exemplify the Nordic model, characterized by high levels of taxation coupled with extensive social welfare programs. This model prioritizes universal access to health care, education, and social services, funded primarily through progressive taxation.

1. Taxation and Redistribution

The Nordic countries employ a robust tax system that redistributes wealth to fund social programs. This progressive taxation model ensures that those with higher incomes contribute a fair share, reducing income inequality and enhancing social cohesion.

2. Universal Social Services

By providing universal access to services, these countries mitigate disparities in health and education. Citizens benefit from comprehensive healthcare and education systems that are funded through taxes, ensuring that all individuals have access to essential services regardless of their socioeconomic status.

3. Lessons for the U.S.

The U.S. could learn from the Nordic approach by exploring progressive taxation models and evaluating the potential for universal social services. Such reforms could help address existing disparities and improve access to critical resources for underserved populations.

Germany: The Social Market Economy

Germany's social market economy strikes a balance between free-market capitalism and social welfare, emphasizing both economic growth and social justice.

1. Cooperative Funding Models

Germany employs cooperative funding approaches, particularly in the areas of renewable energy and social enterprises. Community-owned renewable energy projects demonstrate how collective investment can drive local economies while addressing environmental concerns.

2. Public-Private Partnerships

The German model often incorporates public-private partnerships (PPPs) to fund infrastructure and social programs. These partnerships leverage private sector efficiency while ensuring public accountability and social responsibility.

3. Implications for U.S. Policy

The U.S. could enhance its funding strategies by fostering public-private partnerships, particularly in infrastructure and community development projects. Encouraging cooperative funding initiatives would also promote local engagement and investment in sustainable practices.

Canada's funding framework emphasizes equity and inclusivity, particularly in health and education.

1. Indigenous Funding Initiatives

Canada has implemented specific funding mechanisms aimed at addressing the historical injustices faced by Indigenous communities. These initiatives prioritize self-determination and community-led solutions, ensuring that funding aligns with the needs and goals of Indigenous peoples.

2. Universal Healthcare

Canada's single-payer healthcare system is funded through taxation, providing universal coverage that minimizes out-of-pocket expenses for citizens. This model promotes health equity and reduces disparities in access to care.

3. Lessons for the U.S.

The U.S. could explore more equitable funding models through targeted initiatives for marginalized communities, particularly Indigenous populations. Additionally, examining the feasibility of universal healthcare could lead to more comprehensive health solutions that prioritize equity.

Australia's approach to funding education combines government investment with private contributions, creating a hybrid model.

1. Higher Education Funding

The Australian government employs a unique funding model for higher education that incorporates income-contingent loans. Students can borrow funds for tuition, repaying them based on their future income levels, thus reducing the financial burden on low-income students.

2. Public Funding for Early Childhood Education

Australia invests significantly in early childhood education, recognizing its importance in promoting long-term academic success. This investment is funded through a combination of state and federal resources, ensuring broad access to quality early education.

3. Implications for U.S. Policy

The U.S. could benefit from exploring income-contingent loan systems for higher education, which would alleviate the student debt crisis. Additionally, investing in early childhood education could yield significant long-term benefits for the nation's youth.

One key lesson from international funding models is the importance of flexibility. Countries that adapt their funding approaches to meet the evolving needs of their populations tend to achieve better outcomes.

1. Responsive Funding Mechanisms

For instance, during the COVID-19 pandemic, many countries rapidly adjusted their funding strategies to address immediate health needs. This adaptability allowed for the swift allocation of resources where they were most needed, demonstrating the effectiveness of flexible funding mechanisms.

2. Continuous Evaluation

Regular evaluation and feedback loops are vital for adapting funding strategies. Countries that engage stakeholders in the assessment process are better equipped to refine their approaches and ensure alignment with community needs.

Engaging communities in the funding process is another valuable lesson. Countries that prioritize community involvement tend to create more effective and sustainable initiatives.

1. Participatory Budgeting

Some nations, such as Brazil, have successfully implemented participatory budgeting processes, allowing citizens to directly influence how public funds are allocated. This approach fosters transparency, accountability, and a sense of ownership among community members.

2. Empowering Local Solutions

Empowering communities to design and implement their solutions enhances the relevance and effectiveness of funded programs. This model encourages localized decision-making, which can lead to more culturally appropriate and impactful interventions.

Cross-sector collaboration is essential for addressing complex societal issues. Countries that foster partnerships between government, non-profits, and the private sector tend to develop more comprehensive solutions.

1. Integrated Approaches

For example, the integration of health and social services in many European countries has led to improved health outcomes and reduced costs. By breaking down silos, these nations have created more holistic approaches to funding that address the root causes of societal issues.

2. Leveraging Resources

Collaborating across sectors allows for the pooling of resources, expertise, and innovative ideas. This synergy can enhance the effectiveness of funding initiatives and lead to greater impact.

As the United States contemplates reforming its funding strategies, several implications arise from the lessons learned through international models.

The U.S. could benefit from re-evaluating its funding structures to prioritize equity and flexibility.

1. Progressive Taxation

Adopting a more progressive taxation system could provide the necessary resources to fund essential services and address inequality. This approach would align with the Nordic model and create a more equitable society.

2. Flexible Funding Models

Implementing flexible funding models that allow for rapid reallocation of resources in response to emerging needs would enhance the U.S. response to crises, such as public health emergencies or economic downturns.

Greater community involvement in the funding process could lead to more effective and relevant initiatives.

1. Participatory Approaches

The U.S. could adopt participatory budgeting practices to engage citizens in decision-making processes. This would not only increase transparency but also empower communities to address their unique challenges.

2. Local Solutions

Supporting community-led initiatives and providing funding for local solutions would enhance the relevance and sustainability of programs. This approach recognizes the importance of localized knowledge and expertise in addressing societal issues.

Encouraging collaboration between sectors is vital for developing comprehensive solutions to complex problems.

1. Public-Private Partnerships

Expanding public-private partnerships can enhance resource allocation and efficiency. By leveraging private sector innovation and investment, the U.S. can tackle issues such as infrastructure and social services more effectively.

2. Integrated Service Delivery

Developing integrated service delivery models that combine health, education, and social services can address the multifaceted nature of societal challenges. This approach promotes holistic solutions that consider the interconnectedness of various issues.

Examining global perspectives on funding reveals a wealth of knowledge that can inform U.S. policy. By learning from the successes and challenges faced by other countries, the U.S. can reimagine its funding frameworks to prioritize equity, flexibility, and community engagement. The integration of progressive taxation, participatory approaches, and cross-sector collaboration can lead to more effective funding strategies that address the complex issues facing society today. As we move forward, it is crucial to foster a culture of learning and adaptation, ensuring that funding practices evolve to meet the needs of all citizens.

Chapter 14

A Call to Action

In the intricate tapestry of societal development, funding emerges as a critical thread that influences the fabric of our communities. Throughout this book, we have meticulously examined various dimensions of funding—its sources, allocation methods, and impact on local and national levels. This final chapter serves not only as a summary of our key findings but also as a rallying cry for readers to actively engage in shaping the financial landscapes that affect their lives.

One of the central arguments presented is that funding is not merely a financial resource; it is a means to empower communities, support innovation, and foster equitable growth. We explored how funding disparities often mirror broader societal inequalities, affecting education, healthcare, infrastructure, and social services. Communities with robust funding mechanisms can thrive, while those lacking such support struggle to meet basic needs.

Key Findings:

1. **Disparities in Funding Allocation:**

We highlighted the stark differences in funding allocation across various regions and sectors. Urban areas often receive a disproportionate share of funding compared to rural communities, exacerbating existing inequalities.

This inequity is often a reflection of historical biases and systemic barriers that have persisted over decades.

1. The Role of Government and Philanthropy:

The interplay between government funding and philanthropic contributions was another focal point. While government funding is crucial for public services, philanthropic efforts can fill gaps and drive innovation. However, reliance on philanthropic funding can lead to instability and unpredictability, as these funds may fluctuate based on the priorities of donors rather than the needs of communities.

2. Community Engagement and Empowerment:

Engaging communities in the decision-making processes related to funding is essential. When community members have a voice in how funds are allocated, it leads to more relevant and effective programs. Empowerment fosters ownership, ensuring that initiatives are sustainable and aligned with the actual needs of the population.

3. Advocacy and Policy Change:

Effective advocacy is vital for driving policy changes that address funding inequities. Grassroots movements, coalitions, and advocacy organizations play a critical role in highlighting funding issues and pushing for reforms. The collective power of informed citizens can influence policymakers and lead to significant changes in funding structures.

4. **The Impact of Technology:**

Technology has transformed the way funding is sourced and distributed. Crowdfunding platforms, online petitions, and social media campaigns have democratized fundraising, allowing individuals and communities to mobilize resources more effectively. However, a digital divide remains, and not all communities have equal access to these tools.

The findings presented in this book underscore a fundamental truth: funding shapes our realities. It is imperative that we, as engaged citizens, take an active role in addressing funding disparities and advocating for equitable distribution of resources. This chapter is not just a conclusion; it is an invitation to become part of a larger movement for change.

Engagement is essential for several reasons:

Personal Impact:

The allocation of funds directly affects our lives—our access to quality education, healthcare, public services, and recreational facilities. By understanding and influencing funding decisions, we can create a more equitable society that meets the needs of all its members.

Community Resilience:

When individuals come together to advocate for their community's needs, it fosters resilience. Communities that are proactive in seeking funding solutions are better equipped to face challenges and create sustainable change.

Democratic Responsibility:

Engaging in funding discussions is a civic duty. Democracy thrives on informed participation, and by advocating for transparent and fair funding processes, we strengthen our democratic institutions.

Creating a Legacy:

By participating in funding advocacy, we contribute to building a legacy of equity and justice for future generations. Our actions today can lay the groundwork for a more just and inclusive society tomorrow.

Practical Steps for Advocacy and Involvement

To empower readers to take meaningful action, this section outlines practical steps for advocacy and community involvement in funding issues.

Educate Yourself and Others

Knowledge is power. Start by educating yourself about local and national funding mechanisms. Understand how funding is allocated in your community, the key players involved, and the issues at stake. Share this knowledge with others to foster a collective understanding.

Attend Workshops and Seminars: Participate in workshops focused on funding, advocacy, and community organizing.

Read Reports and Studies: Familiarize yourself with research that highlights funding disparities and their impact.

Create Informational Materials: Develop brochures or online resources that summarize key information for your community.

Build a Coalition

Forming coalitions with like-minded individuals and organizations amplifies your voice. Collaborate with local nonprofits, advocacy groups, and community leaders to create a unified front.

Identify Stakeholders: Reach out to community members, local organizations, and businesses that share your concerns about funding.

Host Community Meetings: Organize gatherings to discuss funding issues and brainstorm solutions. This can help build a network of advocates.

Advocate for Change

Take action to influence local and national funding policies. Here are several strategies to consider:

Write to Elected Officials: Draft letters or emails to your representatives expressing your concerns about funding disparities and advocating for specific policy changes.

Participate in Public Hearings: Attend city council meetings, school board meetings, or legislative sessions to voice your opinions and demand accountability.

Utilize social media: Use platforms like Twitter, Facebook, and Instagram to raise awareness about funding issues. Share stories, statistics, and calls to action to engage a broader audience.

Organize Fundraising Events

If your community lacks resources, consider organizing fundraising events to support local initiatives. This can also raise awareness about funding disparities.

Plan Community Fundraisers: Host events like bake sales, auctions, or charity runs to raise funds for local programs.

Leverage Crowdfunding Platforms: Utilize online platforms to launch campaigns for specific community projects.

Foster Transparency and Accountability

Advocate for transparency in funding processes. Demand that funding allocations are publicly accessible and that communities have a say in how resources are distributed.

Request Public Reports: Encourage local governments to publish reports detailing funding sources and allocations.

Support Accountability Initiatives: Get involved with organizations that monitor and report on funding decisions.

Leverage Technology

Utilize technology to enhance your advocacy efforts. Create engaging online content and use data to support your arguments.

Build a website or Blog: Share information about funding issues, success stories, and ways to get involved.

Use Data Visualization: Present data in visually appealing formats to make the case for funding equity.

Engage with Schools and Educational Institutions

Schools are often at the forefront of funding discussions. Engage with educators, parents, and students to address funding needs in education.

Join School Boards or Committees: Get involved in local school boards to advocate for equitable funding for education.

Organize Educational Workshops: Host events that educate parents and students about funding issues affecting their schools.

Monitor Progress and Celebrate Successes

Advocacy is a long-term commitment. Monitor the progress of your efforts and celebrate successes, no matter how small.

Document Changes: Keep track of policy changes, funding allocations, and community initiatives that result from your advocacy.

Celebrate Achievements: Host events to celebrate milestones and recognize the contributions of community members.

The findings presented throughout this book make it clear that funding is not just a financial issue; it is a deeply intertwined element of social justice and equity. By taking practical steps to advocate for change, we can dismantle barriers, create opportunities, and foster a society where everyone has access to the resources they need to thrive.

Your Involvement matters. Whether you are a seasoned advocate or just beginning to explore the world of funding, there is a role for you in this vital movement. Together, we can transform our communities and ensure that funding is allocated fairly, transparently, and equitably for all. Embrace this call to action, and let us work together for a brighter, more equitable future.

www.ingramcontent.com/pod-product-compliance
Lightning Source LLC
Chambersburg PA
CBHW071408220526
45469CB00004B/1206